WHOLENESS

ACKNOWLEDGMENTS

To Jack Stockman
of Oak Park, Illinois,
for the art work
on the cover.

To Erika Tiepel
of Littleton, Colorado,
for the layout
and design.

To Zondervan Bible Publishers
for permission to use
the NIV text,
The Holy Bible: New International Version
©1973, 1978, 1984 by International Bible Society.
Used by permission of Zondervan Bible Publishers.

WHOLENESS
PUTTING THE PIECES TOGETHER

PETER MENCONI, RICHARD PEACE,
& LYMAN COLEMAN

DEVELOPED BY

SERENDIPITY
H O U S E

DISTRIBUTED BY

NAVPRESS
A MINISTRY OF THE NAVIGATORS

QUESTIONS ABOUT THIS COURSE FOR AN

ENTRY LEVEL SUPPORT GROUP

PURPOSE

1. **What is this course all about?** Becoming a support group while studying the Bible.

SEEKERS/ STRUGGLERS

2. **Who is it for?** Two kinds of people: (a) Seekers who do not know where they are with God but are open to finding out, and (b) Strugglers who are committed to Jesus Christ but need to grow in their faith.

BABY BOOMERS

3. **Who is this course specifically designed for?** While the course is for everyone, the series is primarily written for Baby Boomers.

NEW PEOPLE

4. **Does this mean that I can invite my "non-church" friends?** Absolutely, this is what this group is all about—giving people a chance to restart their spiritual pilgrimage.

STUDY

5. **What are we going to study?** Six causes of interest to wholeness (see inside front cover) and what the Bible has to say about each one.

AUTHORS

6. **Who wrote the material?** Peter Menconi (dentist/Consultant/free-lance writer), Richard Peace (seminary professor and free-lance consultant on media), and Lyman Coleman (group process trainer and writer).

DREAM

7. **What motivated us to write this course?** A dream to offer Baby Boomers and others the chance to investigate the Christian life for a few weeks in a support group.

FIRST SESSION

8. **What do we do at the meetings?** In the first session, you get acquainted and decide on one of two Bible study tracks. In sessions two through seven, you follow the track you chose.

TWO TRACKS

9. **What are the two tracks?** Gospel Study or Epistle Study. The Gospel Study is a more basic, "entry-level" study with a questionnaire with multiple choice options. (None of the options are "right" or "wrong." They are designed to start you thinking.) The Epistle Study has open-ended questions which usually necessitate more involvement in the Scripture text.

5

CHOOSING	**10. Which track of Bible study do you recommend?** The Gospel Study is best for newly-formed groups or groups that are unfamiliar with small group Bible study. The Epistle Study is best for deeper Bible study groups.
BOTH	**11. Can you choose both?** Yes, depending upon your time schedule.

Here's how to decide:

STUDY	APPROXIMATE COMPLETION TIME
Gospel Study only	40–60 minutes
Epistle Study only	40–60 minutes
Gospel and Epistle Study	80–120 minutes

HOMEWORK OPTION	**12. What if we want to do both the Gospel and Epistle Studies but don't have time at the session?** You can spend two weeks on a unit—the Gospel Study the first week and the Epistle Study the next. Or, you can do the Gospel Study in the session and the Epistle Study for homework.
BIBLE KNOWLEDGE	**13. What if you don't know anything about the Bible?** No problem. The Gospel Study is based on a parable or story that stands on its own—to discuss as though you are hearing it for the first time. The Epistle Study comes with complete Reference Notes—to keep you up to speed.

THE FEARLESS FOURSOME
HOW TO OVERCOME GROUP JITTERS!

PROBLEM: A lot of people are afraid of groups.

SOLUTION: Divide into groups of 4 when the time comes for sharing. In 4's the quiet person will be able to talk, and the talkative person will not dominate as much. In fact, in 4's most of the problems of group dynamics will be avoided.

SO: When the time comes for sharing, ask 4 to sit around the dining table, 4 around the kitchen table, and 4 around a folding table in the family room.

REFERENCE NOTES	**14. What is the purpose of the Reference Notes in the Epistle Study?** To help you understand the context of the Bible passage and any difficult words that need to be defined.
LEADERSHIP	**15. Who leads the meetings?** One person can lead for the whole time—or you can rotate the leadership.
RULES	**16. What are the ground rules for the group?**

☐ Priority: While you are in the course, you give the group meetings priority.

☐ Participation: Everyone participates and no one dominates.

☐ Respect: Everyone is given the right to their own opinion and "dumb questions" are encouraged and respected.

☐ Confidentiality: Anything that is said in the meeting is never repeated outside the meeting.

☐ Empty Chair: The group stays open to new people at every meeting as long as they understand the ground rules.

☐ Support: Permission is given to call upon each other in time of need —even in the middle of the night.

CONTINUING	**17. What happens to the group after finishing the course?** The group is free to disband or continue to another course.

> **Orientation:** In the first session, take some time to review the questions and answers on pages 5-7 about this course, especially the RULES for a support group.

SESSION 1
Introduction

Billions of dollars are spent each year in this country by people seeking physical, emotional, and spiritual wholeness. We join health clubs and spas in an attempt to make our bodies fit. Thousands of others pay dearly to have cosmetic surgeons add to and subtract from portions of their bodies. In a similar way, millions use psychiatrists and psychologists to add to and subtract from their "psyches." We are a nation of people seeking purpose—seeking wholeness.

But what is true wholeness and where is it to be found? These are questions which have troubled human beings down through the centuries. Aristotle wrote, "It concerns us to know the purposes we seek in life, for then, like archers aiming at a definite mark, we shall be more likely to attain what we want." Henry David Thoreau was less optimistic about our ability to find wholeness and purpose when he wrote, "the mass of men lead lives of quiet desperation." The art, music and literature of today address our search for wholeness. Popular television shows and movies depict our fragmentation and our struggles to "pick up the pieces."

True wholeness is elusive—yet it can be found. In the following studies we will consider the wholeness offered by Jesus. He offers us wholeness for our bodies, our minds, and our spirits. In a world which is frail, fractured, and frazzled, this truly is good news!

FYI

For Your Information

- About 3 billion dollars a year are spent on vitamins and mineral supplements.

**LEADER:
IF YOU HAVE
MORE THAN SEVEN
AT THE MEETING
SUBDIVIDE
INTO GROUPS OF
FOUR FOR
GREATER
PARTICIPATION
(SEE BOX ON
PAGE 6).**

- According to the Public Health Service, 40% of adult Americans are sedentary. Only 20% exercise vigorously on a regular basis. The other 40% are somewhere in between.

- A recent survey found that our biggest worry is money (58% of respondents). Our second biggest worry is the future (42%), followed by demands on our time (40%), our health (35%), and the health of family or friends (32%).

- Recent medical research has found that a person's emotional health (or, more accurately, the lack of emotional health) can directly affect the body's immune system.

● In a recent survey in a national magazine, 80,000 people responded to the question: do you think spirituality is gaining or losing influence on family life in America? Fifty percent of the respondents believed it was gaining, 14% felt it was staying the same, and 33% believed that spirituality was losing influence on American family life.

OPEN

STEP ONE: This exercise will introduce the topics of the remaining 6 sessions. Answer the following questions and share your responses with your group.

1. Judging from last month's checkbook and datebook entries, in what area of your life do you spend more of your time, money and energy? Accordingly, rank order these concerns from 1 (=least) to 5 (=most):

   _____ physical concerns

   _____ intellectual concerns

   _____ emotional concerns

   _____ spiritual concerns

   _____ relational concerns

2. Which statement best describes how you feel about physical fitness?

   _____ Staying physically fit is very important to me

   _____ I leave physical fitness to the young

   _____ Physical fitness is over-rated in our society

   _____ I worry about it but only exercise sporadically

   _____ When I feel like exercising, I lay down until the feeling goes away

   _____ Physical fitness should be balanced with emotional and spiritual fitness

3. Which statement best describes how you feel about "intellectual stimulation"?

   _____ My mind is closed for repairs

   _____ New ideas interest me but I have little time to pursue them

   _____ I only read comic books, funnies, scandal sheets and other "chewing gum for the mind"

   _____ I grow my mind with a regular reading program

   _____ I am a perpetual student who never stops learning

   _____ "I think, therefore I am"

4. Which statement best describes what part you think emotions should play in a person's life?

____ Emotions are usually not valid and should be ignored

____ Emotions can be good indicators of what is really happening and should be taken seriously

____ Emotions are usually misleading and should be suspect

____ Emotions should be balanced with rational thinking

____ Emotions are mysterious but we can and should learn about them

____ Emotions are useful and necessary in helping us understand ourselves and others better

5. Which concerns—physical, intellectual, emotional, or relational—do you most often confuse or commingle with your spiritual concerns?

____ I am most spiritual when I am physically at ease, tuning into my body and getting bio-rhythmic feedback

____ I am most spiritual when I am emotionally stoic, even-tempered, or carefree

____ I am most spiritual when I am intellectually stimulated with Bible study

____ I am most spiritual when I am relationally at one with others

6. Which statement best describes the relative importance you place on relationships?

____ I believe in J O Y—Jesus, Others, You—in that order

____ If I don't first love myself, how can I love anyone else (even God)?

____ God first loved me, so that I can now love others

____ If we do not love our brothers or sisters in the faith, how can we say we love God?

____ When I love the "least of these" (prisoners, the homeless, the hungry), then am I truly loving God

REFLECT

STEP TWO: As time allows, discuss with your group your agreement or disagreement with the following statements.

- When a man is freed of religion, he has a better chance to live a normal and wholesome life.

    — Sigmund Freud

- I have insisted that there is something radically and systematically wrong with our culture, a flaw that lies deeper than any class or race analysis probes, and which frustrates our best efforts to achieve wholeness. I am convinced it is our ingrained commitment to the scientific picture of nature that hangs us up.

    — Theodore Roszak

SESSION 2
The Paradigm

In this time of scientific and technological sophistication, it is interesting that belief in the supernatural is increasing. Not only do we see an increased interest in supernatural beings in books, movies, and TV shows, but we also are aware that many of our friends and neighbors are "tuning in" to the spiritually unusual. Astrology is no longer easily dismissed in conversation. New Age thinking has made reincarnation and other tenants of Eastern religions increasingly acceptable in our society. Most of these spiritual activities are attempts to reconcile our physical life with our emotional and spiritual dimensions. In short, people want to feel whole and will not settle for the impersonal, scientific explanations for our existence.

In the following Gospel Study, we will see Jesus addressing the issue of human wholeness. He gives us the paradigm by which we should live. A paradigm is a model, standard, or ideal and, in this paradigm Jesus makes it clear that optimum living involves our bodies, minds and spirits. In the Epistle Study, we see how wholeness and unity are achieved within "the body of Christ".

OPTION 1

Gospel Study/The Whole Truth

OPEN

**LEADER:
IF YOU HAVE
MORE THAN SEVEN
AT THE MEETING,
SUBDIVIDE
INTO GROUPS
OF FOUR FOR
GREATER
PARTICIPATION.
(SEE BOX ON
PAGE 6.)**

STEP ONE: Answer the following question and share your responses with your group.

1. Of the following statements, which one describes what you *want* out of life? Which one describes what you are actually *getting* out of life? Where do you feel "cheated"? Why?
   a. I want my life to be as safe and secure as possible
   b. I want to be as emotionally satisfied as possible
   c. I want to be as intellectually aware as possible
   d. I want to be as spiritually mature as possible
   e. I want to "have it all"—physically, intellectually, emotionally, and spiritually

STUDY

STEP TWO: Read Mark 12:28-34 and discuss your responses to the following questions with your group.

   ²⁸*One of the teachers of the law came and heard them debating. Noticing that Jesus had given them a good answer, he asked him, "Of all the commandments, which is the most important?"*

29"The most important one," answered Jesus, "is this: 'Hear O Israel, the Lord our God, the Lord is one. 30Love the Lord your God with all your heart and with all your soul and with all your mind and with all your strength.' 31The second is this: 'Love your neighbor as yourself.' There is no commandment greater than these."

32"Well said, teacher," the man replied. "You are right in saying that God is one and there is no other but him. 33To love him with all your heart, with all your understanding and with all your strength, and to love your neighbor as yourself is more important than all burnt offerings and sacrifices."

34When Jesus saw that he had answered wisely, he said to him, "You are not far from the kingdom of God." And from then on no one dared ask him any more questions.

Mark 12:28–34 NIV

1. If you had a private, "no-holds-barred" opportunity to hit Jesus with a tough question, what would it be?

2. Why do you think one of the teachers questioned Jesus?
   a. He really wanted to know what Jesus thought
   b. He was trying to make Jesus look foolish
   c. He was trying to make himself look intelligent
   c. He was trying to learn more about spiritual truths

3. Why did Jesus give answers from the Old Testament?
   a. Because it was the only source he knew
   b. Because the Law carried authority with the teachers
   c. Because Jesus accepted the Old Testament writings as God-given revelation
   d. Because the answer to the question was found there

4. What is so important about the statement "the Lord is one?"
   a. Monotheism is central to Judaism
   b. Jesus was emphasizing that he was a member of the holy Trinity
   c. God does not want us to worship "other gods"
   d. Other religions are shown to be untrue because they worship multiple gods

5. How and why are we to love God?
   a. We are to love God out of fear
   b. We are to love God because we are commanded to
   c. We are to love God with every part of our being
   d. We are to love God because he loved us first
   e. We are to love God so he doesn't punish us

6. In verse 30, what do we learn about our love for God?
   a. Our love should have an intellectual dimension
   b. Our love should be totally emotional
   c. Our love should involve every "fiber" of our being
   d. Our love has a spiritual dimension
   e. Our love should be all-consuming

7. In verse 31, what do we learn about neighborly love?
   a. If we do not love ourselves, we cannot love others
   b. Love for others reveals whether we truly love God
   c. Relationships are important to God
   d. If we do not love others, we are hypocritical

8. Why did Jesus combine all these commandments into "the greatest commandment"?
   a. He was trying to confuse the teacher
   b. He was clarifying the extent of true love
   c. He was unifying the commandments so they could be understood and applied more clearly
   d. He was emphasizing that love of God and others was central to living

COMMENT: What Jesus asserts here is revolutionary in nature. He makes love the greatest commandment and the highest goal. He connects spirituality to relationships (love God, love others). He calls upon us to use our total human faculties in our love of God. The word *heart* refers to the center of our being, to who we truly are at our core, to our spiritual nature. The word *soul* refers to the seat of our emotions and will, to our inner passions. The word *mind* refers to our reasoning power, to our cognitive ability. The word *strength* refers to physical strength which, in turn, is connected to our bodies. The Greek word used here for "love," *agape*, refers not so much to what we feel as to what we do; love is shown in our behavior. What Jesus has given us, in other words, is a goal to aim at: to become a whole person, with all our facuties—mind, soul, spirit, body, will, and actions—connected together in a unity, with God at the center.

APPLY | **STEP THREE: Answer the following questions and share your responses with your group.**

1. Love has physical, intellectual, emotional, and spiritual dimensions. If you were to assign a percentage to each of these dimensions, how do you think you would assign these percentages? (For example, love is 60% physical, 20% emotional, etc.)
   ____ physical
   ____ emotional
   ____ intellectual
   ____ spiritual

2. Why did you answer the way you did?

OPTION 2

Epistle Study/Wholly Holy

OPEN

STEP ONE: Start with the OPEN question on page 11.

STUDY

STEP TWO: Read Ephesians 2:11-22 and discuss the questions below with your group. If you do not understand a word or phrase, check the Reference Notes on page 15.

¹¹Therefore, remember that formerly you who are Gentiles by birth and called "uncircumcised" by those who call themselves "the circumcision" (that done in the body by the hands of men)— ¹²remember that at that time you were separate from Christ, excluded from citizenship in Israel and foreigners to the covenants of the promise, without hope and without God in the world. ¹³But now in Christ Jesus you who once were far away have been brought near through the blood of Christ.

¹⁴For he himself is our peace, who has made the two one and has destroyed the barrier, the dividing wall of hostility, ¹⁵by abolishing in his flesh the law with its commandments and regulations. His purpose was to create in himself one new man out of the two, thus making peace, ¹⁶and in this one body to reconcile both of them to God through the cross, by which he put to death their hostility. ¹⁷He came and preached peace to you who were far away and peace to those who were near. ¹⁸For through him we both have access to the Father by one Spirit.

¹⁹Consequently, you are no longer foreigners and aliens, but fellow citizens with God's people and members of God's household, ²⁰built on the foundation of the apostles and the prophets, with Christ Jesus himself as the chief cornerstone. ²¹In him the whole building is joined together and rises to become a holy temple in the Lord. ²²And in him you too are being built together to become a dwelling in which God lives by his Spirit.

Ephesians 2:11-22 NIV

1. In what social circles or times of your life have you felt "out of it"—like a stranger in a strange land?

2. What were the major differences between Jews and Gentiles?

3. Before Christ came, why were the Gentiles considered "foreigners and aliens"?

4. How did Christ reconcile the Jews and the Gentiles into "one new man" thus bringing peace to the world?

5. What does it mean to be a "member of God's household"? What are some of the rights and responsibilities that go with this membership?

6. What role does the Holy Spirit play in bringing unity to the body of Christ?

7. In what practical ways are we made whole when included in the "body of Christ"?

REFLECT

STEP THREE: As time allows, discuss with your group your agreement or disagreement with the following statements.

- We live in a "fast food" culture. We are overfed and undernourished on almost every level of existence: physical, emotional, intellectual and spiritual.

— *Albert M. Wells Jr.*

- God is the whole reason we live, and knowing Him is to be our goal, not social approval or glandular satisfaction. He knows our needs; He has sent us a Comforter. And a life developed cheerfully and fully in the way God intended will bring the rewards that only God can give.

— *Barbara Sroka*

APPLY

STEP FOUR: Answer the following questions and share your responses with your group.

1. In what ways has your relationship with Christ affected your development of wholeness?

2. In what practical ways has being a member of "the body of Christ" affected your development of wholeness?

REFERENCE
NOTES

Summary . . . Paul moves from the problem of human alienation from God (2:1-10) to the related problem of alienation between people themselves (2:11-22). In both cases the problem is hostility (or enmity). In both cases, Christ is the one who, through his death, brings peace—first between God and people, but then, also, between human enemies.

The particular focus of this section is on the deep hostility between Jew and Gentile. Paul begins by reminding the Gentiles of their five-fold alienation from God's plan for the world (vv. 11-12). But he then goes on to describe how Jesus' death overcame all that (vv. 13-18). Jesus *abolished* the law which divided (people from God; Jew from Gentile); he *created* a new humanity; and he *reconciled* this new "race" to God. Paul concludes by describing, through three metaphors, (kingdom, family, temple), the new reality which has emerged (vv. 19-22).

15

v. 11 **remember** . . . In verses 1–3, Paul reminded his Gentile readers that once they were trapped in their transgressions and sins, and so were spiritually dead and alienated from God. Here in verse 11 he asks them to remember that once they were also isolated from all the *blessings of God.* In verses 1–3 the focus is on being cut off from God himself, while in verses 11–13, the focus is on being cut off from God's kingdom and God's people.

formerly . . . The focus in verses 11–12 is on what the Gentiles *once were,* prior to the beginning of their spiritual odyssey.

"uncircumcised" . . . This is a derogatory slur by which Gentiles were mocked. With this contemptuous nickname the Jews were saying that the Gentiles' lack of "God's mark" on their bodies put them absolutely outside of God's kingdom; so they were to be despised.

"the circumcision" . . . This is how Jews thought of themselves and was a term used with pride. Circumcision was the sign given to Abraham by which the covenant people were to be marked. This made the Jew different and special.

v. 12 . . . Paul describes the five disabilities faced by the Gentile world prior to Christ. They were "Christless, stateless, friendless, hopeless, and Godless" (Hendriksen).

separate from Christ . . . In contrast to the great blessings (described in chapter 1 and in 2:4–10) which come as a result of being "in Christ," at one time the Gentiles were outside Christ. That is, they had no hope of a coming Messiah who would make all things right. Instead, they considered themselves to be caught up in the deadly cycle of history which led nowhere. This separation from the hope of a Messiah was the first liability faced by Gentiles.

excluded from citizenship . . . Gentiles were not part of God's kingdom. Israel was a nation founded by God, consisting of his people; and Gentiles were outside that reality. This was their second liability.

foreigners to the covenants . . . Not only did Gentiles have no part in God's kingdom, they also stood outside all the amazing agreements (covenants) God made with his people (see, for example, Exodus 6:6–8; Deuteronomy 28:9–14). This is the third liability.

without hope . . . During this particular historical era the Roman world experienced a profound loss of hope. The first century was inundated with mystery cults, all promising salvation from this despair. Living in fear of demons, people felt themselves to be mere playthings of the capricious gods. This lack of hope in the face of fear was the fourth liability.

without God . . . This is not to say that Gentiles were atheists (even though the word used here is *atheos*). On the contrary, they worshiped scores of deities. The problem was that they had no *effective* knowledge of the one true God. This is the final liability.

v. 13 **But now . . .** This the second great "But" which signals God's intervention into a seemingly hopeless situation. The first use of "But" in this fashion is found in 2:4–5 where Paul describes what God has done in the face of universal sin and bondage.

through the blood of Christ . . . Paul pinpoints how this great change occurred. It is as a result of Jesus' death on the cross that union with Christ is possible (see 1:7).

v. 14 **our peace . . .** Jesus brings *peace,* that is, he creates harmony between human beings and God. He also creates harmony between human beings. He draws together those who consider each other to be enemies. He does this by being the one who stands between the alienated parties, bridging the gap that separates them.

the dividing wall of hostility . . . Paul has in mind an actual wall which existed in the temple in Jerusalem. The temple itself was built on an elevated area. The inner sanctuary was surrounded by the Court of the Priests. Beyond this was the Court of Israel (for men only) and then the Court of the Women. All these courts were on the same level as the temple; and each had a different degree of exclusivity. Ringing all the courts and some 19 steps below was the Court of the Gentiles. Here Gentiles could gaze up at the temple. But they could not approach it. They were cut off by a stone wall ("the dividing wall") bearing signs that warned in Greek and Latin that trespassing foreigners would be killed. Paul himself knew well this prohibition. He had nearly been lynched by a mob of Jews who were told he had taken a Gentile into the temple.

hostility . . . The ancient world abounded in hostility. There was enmity between Jew and Gentile, Greek and barbarian, men and women, slave and free. Christ ends each form of hostility.

vv. 15-16 . . . By means of three key verbs ("abolish," "create," and "reconcile") Paul describes the three accomplishments of Christ on the cross whereby he destroys "the dividing wall of hostility."

v. 15 **the law with its commandments and regulations** . . . The primary reference is to the thousands of rules and regulations which were in existence at the time of Christ by which Jewish leaders sought to define the "Law of Moses." The belief was that only by keeping all these rules could one be counted "good" and therefore have fellowship with God.

one new man . . . In the place of divided humanity, Jesus creates a whole new quality of being, a new humanity, as it were. This does not mean that Jews became Gentiles nor that Gentiles became Jews. Both became Christians, "the third race" (see also Galatians 3:28 and Colossians 3:11).

v. 16 **reconcile** . . . This word means "to bring together estranged parties." In verse 14 the emphasis is on reconciling Jew to Gentile. Here the reference is to bringing both Jew and Gentile together with God.

v. 17 **He came and preached peace** . . . Since such peace was possible only through the cross, this reference is probably to Jesus' post-resurrection appearances. His first words to the stunned apostles after his resurrection were, in fact, "Peace be with you" (John 20:19).

v. 18 **access** . . . In Greek, one form of this word is used to describe an individual whose job it is to usher a person into the presence of the king. Indeed, not only did Jesus open the way back to God (by his death humanity was *reconciled* to God), he continues to provide the means whereby an ongoing and continuing relationship is possible.

vv. 19-22 . . . To describe the achievements of Jesus, Paul uses three images: that of God's kingdom, God's family, and God's temple.

v. 19 **Consequently** . . . Paul will now describe the results of this threefold work of Christ on the cross.

foreigners . . . Non-resident aliens who were disliked by the native population and often held in suspicion.

aliens . . . They are residents in a foreign land. They pay taxes but have no legal standing and few rights.

fellow citizens . . . Whereas once the Gentiles were "excluded from citizenship in Israel" (v. 12), now they are members of God's kingdom. They now "belong."

members of God's household . . . In fact, they do not merely have a new legal status ("citizens"), their relationship is far more intimate. They have become family.

v. 20 **the foundation of the apostles and prophets . . .** Since both apostles and prophets are teachers, this phrase could mean that the Church rests on the teaching of both the Old Testament (prophets) and the New Testament (apostles). However, since the order is reversed, it probably means that the Church rests on the teaching of the apostles and the New Testament prophets that followed them.

cornerstone . . . That stone which rested firmly on the foundation and tied two walls together, giving each its correct alignment. The temple in Jerusalem had massive cornerstones (one was nearly 40 feet long). The image might be of Jesus holding together Jew and Gentile, Old Testament and New Testament.

v. 21 **joined together . . .** Used by a mason to describe how two stones were prepared so that they would bond tightly together.

temple . . . The new temple is not like the old one, carved out of dead stone, beautiful but forbidding and exclusive. Rather, it is alive all over the world, inclusive of all, made up of the individuals in whom God dwells.

SESSION 3
Physical

We do not usually appreciate our physical health until we lose it. It may only be the aches, nausea, and general malaise of the flu which gets us to temporarily think about how wonderful physical health is. Or it may be a chronic, debilitating condition which permanently alters our lives and causes us to forget what physical wholeness even felt like. Whatever our current condition, it is important that we be attentive to our physical health and well-being.

We also tend to forget that there is a connection between our physical and our spiritual health. Apart from anything else, when we are ill we cannot be involved in ministry in the same way as when we are healthy. Furthermore, our emotions are often off-key then, and our mind doesn't work as well as it normally does. Have you ever tried to pray when you have a fever? God has given us wonderful bodies with amazing capabilities and it is part of our spiritual responsibility to keep them in good condition to the best of our ability.

**LEADER:
IF YOU HAVE
MORE THAN SEVEN
AT THE MEETING,
SUBDIVIDE
INTO GROUPS OF
FOUR FOR
GREATER
PARTICIPATION
(SEE BOX ON
PAGE 6).**

Jesus understood the importance of physical health. Not only did he heal many who were sick and debilitated, but he also understood the importance of taking care of a healthy body. In the following Gospel passage, we will see that Jesus encouraged his disciples to get away and rest. He also recognized that the body needs proper food and nourishment. He modeled for us the importance of being good stewards of our bodies. In the Epistle Study, the Apostle Paul underscores the importance of our bodies as "the temple of the Holy Spirit." Both passages place the responsibility for the "preventive maintenance" of our physical bodies squarely on our shoulders.

OPTION 1

Gospel Study/Physical Education

OPEN

STEP ONE: Answer the following questions and share your responses with your group.

1. How would you assess your physical health? On what basis?

_____ excellent   _____ good   _____ fair   _____ poor

2. Which one of the following best describes how you treat your physical health?

____ I worry about it

____ I don't give it a second thought

____ I do what I can to stay healthy

____ I probably am not as conscientious as I should be

____ I take it for granted

____ I give it top priority

3. What do you do to safeguard your physical health?

STUDY

STEP TWO: Read Mark 6:30-44 and discuss your responses to the following questions with your group.

³⁰The apostles gathered around Jesus and reported to him all they had done and taught. ³¹Then, because so many people were coming and going that they did not even have a chance to eat, he said to them, "Come with me by yourselves to a quiet place and get some rest."

³²So they went away by themselves in a boat to a solitary place. ³³But many who saw them leaving recognized them and ran on foot from all the towns and got there ahead of them. ³⁴When Jesus landed and saw a large crowd, he had compassion on them, because they were like sheep without a shepherd. So he began teaching them many things. ³⁵By this time it was late in the day, so his disciples came to him. "This is a remote place," they said, "and it's already very late. ³⁶Send the people away so they can go to the surrounding countryside and villages and buy themselves something to eat."

³⁷But he answered, "You give them something to eat."

They said to him, "That would take eight months of a man's wages! Are we to go and spend that much on bread and give it to them to eat?"

³⁸"How many loaves do you have?" he asked. "Go and see."

When they found out, they said, "Five—and two fish."

³⁹Then Jesus directed them to have all the people sit down in groups on the green grass. ⁴⁰So they sat down in groups of hundreds and fifties. ⁴¹Taking the five loaves and the two fish and looking up to heaven, he gave thanks and broke the loaves. Then he gave them to his disciples to set before the people. He also divided the two fish among them all. ⁴²They all ate and were satisfied, ⁴³and the disciples picked up twelve basketfuls of broken pieces of bread and fish. ⁴⁴The number of the men who had eaten was five thousand.

Mark 6:30-44 NIV

1. If you were all set to enjoy a well-deserved vacation, what experiences might ruin it for you?
   a. Running out of money, gas, food, or film
   b. Running into acquaintances from back home
   c. Running into mosquitos/jellyfish/ants
   d. Running to keep pace with some itinerary
   e. Running around with undone work from the office

2. What do we learn about the relationship between Jesus and his disciples?
   a. They questioned Jesus' judgement
   b. They did whatever he asked them to do
   c. Jesus looked out for their welfare
   d. Jesus directed the disciples' itinerary

3. Why did Jesus want the disciples to find a quiet place and rest?
   a. Because he knew they were tired
   b. Because Jesus wanted some time alone
   c. Because Jesus understood the need for physical rest and restoration
   d. Because Jesus was annoyed with the crowd
   e. Because they had just returned from an exhausting time of ministry

4. In verse 34, what was Jesus' reaction to the crowd?
   a. He was overwhelmed
   b. He was angry because they had followed him
   c. He was compassionate and loving
   d. He was upset because he did not get a chance to rest

5. How did Jesus' thinking differ from the thinking of the disciples?
   a. Jesus saw the crowd as needy; the disciples saw the crowd as a problem
   b. Jesus had control of the situation; the disciples thought the situation was out of control
   c. Jesus was solution-oriented; the disciples were problem-oriented
   d. Jesus had a spiritual perspective; the disciples had an earthly perspective

6. How do you think you would have reacted if Jesus asked you to feed the crowd with five loaves and two fish?
   a. I would have simply done what he instructed
   b. I would have said, "You have got to be kidding!"
   c. I would have questioned his reasoning
   d. I would have asked him what he knew that I didn't

7. Why do you think Jesus performed this miracle?
   a. He wanted to show his power
   b. He wanted to teach the disciples something
   c. He wanted simply to feed hungry people
   d. He wanted to make it clear that he was the Messiah

8. What do we learn about Jesus in these verses?
   a. Jesus is a compassionate person
   b. Jesus liked to tease his disciples
   c. Jesus liked big spectacles
   d. Jesus had miraculous power
   e. Jesus considered physical wholeness to be important
   f. Jesus knew exactly what he was doing
   g. Jesus was "laid back"

APPLY | **STEP THREE: Answer the following questions and share your responses with your group.**

1. How do you think you would react if your physical health and wholeness were lost?

2. Imagine for a moment that you could no longer walk. How would this change your life? How would it affect your relationships?

3. If God wanted you to change one thing about the way you treat your body, what do you think it would be?

OPTION 2 | # Epistle Study/Body Language

OPEN | STEP ONE: Start with the OPEN questions on page 20-21.

STUDY | **STEP TWO: Read 1 Corinthians 6:12-20** and share your responses to the following questions with your group. If you do not understand a word or phrase, check the Reference Notes on page 25.

12"Everything is permissible for me"—but not everything is beneficial. "Everything is permissible for me"—but I will not be mastered by anything. 13"Food for the stomach and the stomach for food"—but God will destroy them both. The body is not meant for sexual immorality, but for the Lord, and the Lord for the body. 14By his power God raised the Lord from the dead, and he will raise us also. 15Do you not know that your bodies are members of Christ himself? Shall I then take the members of Christ and unite them with a prostitute? Never! 16Do you not know that he who unites himself with a prostitute is one with her in body? For it is said, "The two will become one flesh." 17But he who unites himself with the Lord is one with him in spirit.

18Flee from sexual immorality. All other sins a man commits are outside his body, but he who sins sexually sins against his own body. 19Do you not know that your body is a temple of the Holy Spirit, who is in you, whom you have received from God? You are not your own; 20you were bought at a price. Therefore honor God with your body.

1 Corinthians 6:12–20 NIV

1. As you age, what will go first; your appetite for food or sex? Why do you think so?

2. In what way is "everything permissible" for the Christian?

3. How does God view our bodies?

4. In what ways can Christians "prostitute" their bodies?

5. What is the significance of the fact that our "bodies are members of Christ himself"?

6. What makes the sin of sexual immorality unique?

7. If our bodies are "temples of the Holy Spirit," how should we treat them?

8. In what practical ways can we "honor God with our bodies"?

REFLECT

STEP THREE: As time allows, discuss with your group your agreement or disagreement with the following statements.

- We take excellent care of our bodies, which we have for only a lifetime; yet we let our souls shrivel, which we will have for eternity.

— Billy Graham

- Usually any one or all of the sexual difficulties that a person experiences stem from inadequate functioning of the most important sexual organ of them all—the head, which controls the mind, the attitudes, and the emotions influencing behavior.

— *Barbara Chesser*

APPLY

STEP FOUR: Answer the following questions and share your responses with your group.

1. In what ways do you experience a conflict between your mind and your body?

2. In what practical ways can you use your body to serve God?

REFERENCE NOTES

Summary . . . Paul now tackles head-on the confusion that exists in the newly-formed Corinthian church over the question of sexuality. This is actually Part 2 of that discussion. In 5:1-13 he addressed a specific problem (incest). Here he discusses another problem (prostitution) and by so doing lays down some general (negative) guidelines. In chapter 7 he will discuss the positive side of sexuality when he examines marriage.

vv. 12-13 . . . Paul begins with two quotations which probably reflect the views of the Corinthians. While not denying these outright, Paul does take to task the conclusions people have drawn from these maxims.

v. 12 **"Everything is permissible for me"** . . . This was probably the slogan of a libertarian party at Corinth, which felt that since the body was insignificant (in comparison with the "spirit") it did not really matter what one did. In one sense, this slogan is true. It defines the nature of Christian freedom and Paul does not disagree with it. He does, however, take issue with how the slogan has come to be used; i.e., as an excuse for indulgent and promiscuous behavior. He argues that while everything may be permissible, not everything is good, much less beneficial.

not everything is beneficial . . . "Christian existence is dependent not upon the observance of rules, whether Jewish, pagan, gnostic, or Christian—in origin, but solely and entirely on the free gracious activity of God, who out of pure love accepts even those who break his own laws. It does not follow, however, that it is a good and profitable thing for a Christian to exercise his freedom in an irresponsible way (cf. Galatians 5:13; also 1 Peter 2:16). In truth, only love, and actions based on love, are expedient for the people of God, since only these build up (8:1). And though obedience to law is now completely discounted as a means of justification, God's law still stands (9:21), or rather has been simplified and reinforced in Christ (the law of Christ, Galatians 6:2), and may be regarded as marking out for men not a way of salvation but ways that are inexpedient, because they will lead inevitably to the collapse of society and the ruin of men's lives. Christian freedom must be limited by regard for others" (Barrett).

mastered . . . To indulge one's appetites in unsuitable ways is to put oneself under the *power* of that appetite and to open the possibility of slavery to a harmful habit. So, in fact, such license is not really Christian liberty because it produces bondage!

v. 13 **"Food for the stomach"** . . . Here also in this second slogan the low view of the gnostics towards the body asserts itself. Paul does not directly dispute this slogan either. Christians are not bound by food laws. Diet is a matter of indifference—especially in that it has no impact on one's salvation.

body . . . The stomach is one thing (it will pass away in the natural course of things) but the body is something else (it will live on). "Body" means for Paul not just bones and tissues but the whole person. "Sexual intercourse, unlike eating, is an act of the whole person, and therefore participates not in the transiency of material members, but in the continuity of the resurrection of life" (Barrett).

not meant for sexual immorality . . . Paul now qualifies his acceptance of the slogan. It appears, Barrett suggests, that the Corinthians were arguing that in the same way that it was permissible for Christians to satisfy their physical appetite without regard to law, so too they had the right to satisfy their sexual appetite with the same disregard of law. This Paul emphatically denies.

v. 14 **raise us also** . . . In fact the body will be resurrected, as was the Lord's body. (His was not a "spiritual" resurrection, Jesus' *body* was missing from the tomb.)

v. 15 . . . Since the body of the Christian belongs to the Lord and is for his use, it is inconceivable ("Never!") that it be handed over to a prostitute.

prostitute . . . Paul may not have in mind just prostitutes in general (they were numerous in a port city like Corinth) but temple prostitutes in particular. The Corinthians may have been arguing for the "right" to engage in sexually-oriented religious activities.

26

v. 16 **Do you not know . . .** This is no new principle which Paul proposes, as he shows by quoting Genesis 2:24.

> **unites . . .** "Joined together." In its literal use this word referred to gluing things together. In its metaphorical sense here, it points to the strong bonding between two people that takes place as a result of intercourse. Intercourse is not merely an inconsequential physical act. In fact, it is akin to the bonding between the believer and the Lord, as Paul shows in verse 17 where he uses this same word.

> **flesh . . .** Such uniting with a prostitute makes the two one *flesh*. This stands in contrast to becoming *one in spirit* with God (v. 17).

v. 18 **flee . . .** The temptation to sexual sin was so overwhelming in Corinth that Paul uses this strong verb by way of command.

> **sexual immorality . . .** The Corinthians, not unexpectedly, given the nature of life in Corinth, were confused about their sexuality. In chapter 7 it appears that many felt marriage should be avoided and certainly sexual intercourse was to be shunned between marriage partners. So here the proposition which Paul is disputing might be that since it was the duty of a husband to keep his wife "pure," if necessary he could occasionally find sexual satisfaction with a harlot (Barrett).

> **sins against his own body . . .** "My explanation is that (Paul) does not completely deny that there are other sins which also bring dishonor and disgrace upon our bodies, but that he is simply saying that these other sins do not leave anything like the same filthy stain on our bodies as fornication does" (Calvin).

v. 19 **. . .** In 3:10 Paul pointed out that the church was the dwelling place of the Holy Spirit. Here he points to the parallel truth: so too is the individual believer.

v. 20 **bought at a price . . .** The image is of ransoming slaves from their bondage. In the same way Christ paid the ransom price in order that Christians be free from the bondage of sin. Out of sheer gratitude, a Christian ought to flee sin. Out of sheer common sense, he/she should flee sin lest he/she fall back into bondage.

SESSION 4
Intellectual

While some people contend that you are what you eat, to a greater extent you are what you think. Woodrow Wilson, one of our former presidents, went so far as to say: "He that will not command his thoughts will soon lose command of his actions." What you think about throughout the day usually determines how you act throughout the day. If you spend most of your time thinking about how to make money, it is likely that much of your activity will be directed toward making money.

An equally important question has to do with our mind set. When we look out upon the events around us, how do we make sense out of them? Do we use secular grids to assess situations; or is our world-view conditioned by our Christian commitment? In our complex society, we have many ideologies and philosophies vying for our acceptance. It becomes imperative to build our world view on Christian truth. This will involve on-going study and reflection.

In the following studies, we see Jesus and the Apostle Paul presenting the truth and wisdom of God's kingdom. We are challenged to examine the claims of Jesus as the Messiah and Son of God. We are also challenged to examine and experience the spiritual wisdom which brings ultimate wholeness. We have a choice. We can fill our "open minds" with the "wisdom of this age," or we can embrace the reality of the risen Christ.

OPTION 1

Gospel Study/Free Thinker

OPEN

STEP ONE: Answer the following questions and share your responses with your group.

**LEADER:
IF YOU HAVE
MORE THAN SEVEN
AT THE MEETING,
SUBDIVIDE
INTO GROUPS OF
FOUR FOR
GREATER
PARTICIPATION
(SEE BOX ON
PAGE 6).**

1. Where did you derive *most* of your ideas about life? (choose three)
   - ____ my parents
   - ____ college professors
   - ____ other relatives
   - ____ TV, movies, newspapers, etc.
   - ____ traveling widely
   - ____ "trial and error"
   - ____ my friends
   - ____ church/ministers
   - ____ reading books
   - ____ the Bible
   - ____ reflection about life

2. Which of the above sources have *least* influenced your ideas about life?

STEP TWO: Read John 8:12–41 and discuss your responses to the following questions with your group.

¹²When Jesus spoke again to the people, he said, "I am the light of the world. Whoever follows me will never walk in darkness, but will have the light of life."

¹³The Pharisees challenged him, "Here you are, appearing as your own witness; your testimony is not valid."

¹⁴Jesus answered, "Even if I testify on my own behalf, my testimony is valid, for I know where I came from and where I am going. But you have no idea where I come from or where I am going. ¹⁵You judge by human standards; I pass judgment on no one. ¹⁶But if I do judge, my decisions are right, because I am not alone. I stand with the Father, who sent me. ¹⁷In your own Law it is written that the testimony of two men is valid. ¹⁸I am one who testifies for myself; my other witness is the Father, who sent me."

¹⁹Then they asked him, "Where is your father?"

"You do not know me or my Father," Jesus replied. "If you knew me, you would know my Father also." ²⁰He spoke these words while teaching in the temple area near the place where the offerings were put. Yet no one seized him, because his time had not yet come.

²¹Once more Jesus said to them, "I am going away, and you will look for me, and you will die in your sin. Where I go, you cannot come."

²²This made the Jews ask, "Will he kill himself? Is that why he says, 'Where I go, you cannot come'?"

²³But he continued, "You are from below; I am from above. You are of this world; I am not of this world. ²⁴I told you that you would die in your sins; if you do not believe that I am the one I claim to be, you will indeed die in your sins."

²⁵"Who are you?" they asked.

"Just what I have been claiming all along," Jesus replied. ²⁶"I have much to say in judgment of you. But he who sent me is reliable, and what I have heard from him I tell the world."

²⁷They did not understand that he was telling them about his Father. ²⁸So Jesus said, "When you have lifted up the Son of Man, then you will know that I am the one I claim to be and that I do nothing on my own but speak just what the Father has taught me. ²⁹The one who sent me is with me; he has not left me alone, for I always do what pleases him." ³⁰Even as he spoke, many put their faith in him.

³¹To the Jews who had believed him, Jesus said, "If you hold to my teaching, you are really my disciples. ³²Then you will know the truth, and the truth will set you free."

33They answered him, "We are Abraham's descendants and have never have been slaves of anyone. How can you say that we shall be set free?"

34Jesus replied, "I tell you the truth, everyone who sins is a slave to sin. 35Now a slave has no permanent place in the family, but a son belongs to it forever. 36So if the Son sets you free, you will be free indeed. 37I know you are Abraham's descendants. Yet you are ready to kill me, because you have no room for my word. 38I am telling you what I have seen in the Father's presence, and you do what you have heard from your father."

39"Abraham is our father," they answered.

"If you were Abraham's children," said Jesus, "then you would do the things Abraham did. 40As it is, you are determined to kill me, a man who has told you the truth that I heard from God. Abraham did not do such things. 41You are doing the things your own father does."

"We are not illegitimate children," they protested. "The only Father we have is God himself."

John 8:12-41 NIV

1. How would you define yourself in terms of your ancestral roots? (Where did your ancestors come from? How did they get to this country?)

2. According to these verses, who did Jesus say that he was?
   a. The Messiah
   b. The Son of God
   c. The light of the world
   d. The Son of Man

3. Why did Jesus say that his claims were valid?
   a. Because he was above the Law
   b. Because he had come from God—his Father
   c. Because he was smarter than the Pharisees
   d. Because he was the Messiah

4. What standard should be used to determine if Jesus is the Son of God and Savior of the world?
   a. Jesus should be accepted or rejected totally on faith
   b. Jesus should be accepted or rejected by the evidence
   c. Jesus should be accepted or rejected by what we want out of life
   d. Jesus should be accepted or rejected after examining his whole message

5. What did Jesus say about our ability to understand and think in spiritual terms?
   a. Spiritual thinking comes naturally to most of us
   b. Spiritual thinking takes faith
   c. Spiritual thinking should be considered as valid as other thinking
   d. Without spiritual thinking we cannot know the reality of life and death

6. Why do you think people believe in Jesus?
   a. Because they need a "crutch" to lean on
   b. Because he obviously is the Son of God
   c. Because he offers "fire insurance"
   d. Because the Holy Spirit brings them to respond in faith

7. How can we "know the truth"?
   a. By studying Scripture
   b. By examining all the evidence
   c. By believing in Christ and following his teachings
   d. By asking the Holy Spirit to reveal it to us

8. How can the truth set us free?
   a. By helping us understand what life is about
   b. By giving us a spiritual perspective on life
   c. By giving us an advantage over others
   d. By giving us eternal life
   e. By letting us do whatever we want

APPLY

STEP THREE: Answer the following questions and discuss your responses with your group.

1. Do you think Christianity has an intellectual basis? If so, why? If not, why not?

2. Do you think a person must put their intellect aside to believe in Jesus Christ? Explain your response.

3. How can intellectual thinking and spiritual thinking be combined to make us more whole?

OPTION 2

Epistle Study/Open Mind

OPEN

STEP ONE: Start with the OPEN questions on page 28.

STUDY

STEP TWO: Read 1 Corinthians 2:6-16 and discuss the following questions with your group. If you do not understand a word or phrase, check the Reference Notes on page 33.

⁶We do, however, speak a message of wisdom among the mature, but not the wisdom of this age or of the rulers of this age, who are coming to nothing. ⁷No, we speak of God's secret wisdom, a wisdom that has been hidden and that God destined for our glory before time began. ⁸None of the rulers of this age understood it, for if they had, they would not have crucified the Lord of glory. ⁹However, as it is written:

> *"No eye has seen,*
> *no ear has heard,*
> *no mind has conceived*
> *what God has prepared for those who love him"—*

¹⁰but God has revealed it to us by his Spirit.

The Spirit searches all things, even the deep things of God. ¹¹For who among men knows the thoughts of a man except the man's spirit within him? In the same way no one knows the thoughts of God except the Spirit of God. ¹²We have not received the spirit of the world but the Spirit who is from God, that they may understand what God has freely given us. ¹³This is what we speak, not in words taught us by human wisdom but in words taught by the Spirit, expressing spiritual truths in spiritual words. ¹⁴The man without the Spirit does not accept the things that come from the Spirit of God, for they are foolishness to him, and he cannot understand them, because they are spiritually discerned. ¹⁵The spiritual man makes judgments about all things, but he himself is not subject to any man's judgment:

> *¹⁶"For who has known the mind of the Lord*
> *that he may instruct him?"*

But we have the mind of Christ.

1 Corinthians 2:6-16 NIV

1. In what areas might some consider you a "specialist"? How did you achieve this status?

2. How would you describe "the wisdom of this age"?

3. How does God's wisdom differ from human wisdom?

4. How would you interpret verse 9 (Isa. 64:4)?

5. How can we know the "deep things of God"?

6. How should the thinking of a Christian differ from the thinking of a non-Christian?

7. What makes a person's thinking foolish?

8. In practice, how can we have "the mind of Christ"?

REFLECT

STEP THREE: As time allows, discuss with your group your agreement or disagreement with the following statements.

- Change your thoughts and you change your world.

  — *Norman Vincent Peale*

- The relationship of a man's soul to God is best evidenced by those things that occupy his thoughts.

  — *Kenneth L. Dodge*

APPLY

STEP FOUR: Answer the following questions and share your responses with your group.

1. What part does your intellect play in your acceptance or rejection of Christ?

2. Why do you think it is important to comprehend spiritual truths?

3. What part should the Holy Spirit play in our personal understanding of spiritual truth?

REFERENCE NOTES

Summary . . . Paul will now qualify what he just said about his rejection of human wisdom (vv. 4–5). There is, in fact, a legitimate "message of wisdom," but, as he shows in verses 6–16 it comes from God and is discerned only by those who have the Spirit.

v. 6 **a message of wisdom . . .** Paul will now use *sophia* (wisdom) in a positive way to describe God's plan of salvation. This use of *sophia* stands in sharp contrast to that in 1:17 where wisdom is seen as persuasive human eloquence and to the uses in 1:18-25 where wisdom is evil because it makes human aspiration the criterion for truth.

among . . . Paul did not speak as some sort of elevated leader with insight no one else had. Rather the "message of wisdom" was shared in the context of the insights of other mature Christians who also had something to add (12:8).

mature . . . To be mature is to be a full-grown adult in the faith, a potential which all Christians have (Colossians 1:28) though not all experience (3:1).

but not . . . Paul first describes what God's wisdom is *not*: it is not derived from either the self-serving philosophy of fallen men and women nor from the presuppositions of the rulers.

wisdom of this age . . . In biblical thought there are two ages; "this age" in which sin and evil exist and "the age to come" when God's kingdom will be present and visible. Wisdom of this age is person-centered, and corrupted by rebellion against God—despite how it may appear on the surface.

rulers of this age . . . Sometimes this term is used to describe evil supernatural powers thought to control human destiny, but here it seems that Paul is referring to human leaders, since in verse 8 he says that these are the ones who crucified Jesus, and since the contrast in this whole passage is between the Christian (who has the Spirit), and the non-Christian (who does not).

v. 7 **God's secret wisdom . . .** In contrast to the "wisdom of the world" in which the attempt is made to show by persuasive words of rhetoric how "obvious" and "reasonable" it is, no one could have guessed God's plan. Even when it was revealed, many shunned it as "foolish" and/or scandalous (1:23).

secret . . . This is not a secret (literally *mystery*) in the sense of something that is cryptic and beyond human understanding. Rather, it means something God alone knew (it was once hidden) but which he has now revealed.

hidden . . . In the sense that God's plan of salvation was only just recently disclosed (Paul is writing some 20–30 years after the crucifixion) via the death and resurrection of Jesus, prior to which God's full intentions were known by no one.

destined for our glory . . . God always intended that humanity be redeemed and become a part of his glorious kingdom.

v. 8 **understood . . .** No one understood that Christ crucified was to be God's agent of redemption.

v. 9 **. . .** Paul quotes Isaiah 64:4 loosely, probably from memory.

v. 10 **revealed to us . . .** That which was hidden from the non-Christian rulers (v. 8) has now been made clear to the Christian.

by his Spirit . . . The insight referred to in verses 6–9 came not as a result of reasoning but as a result of revelation.

The Spirit searches all things . . . In Corinth, the idea was that you could by means of philosophy search out the nature of God. Paul indicates that only the Spirit himself communicates accurate knowledge about God.

v. 11 **. . .** Paul uses an analogy to explain his point.

v. 12 **the spirit of the world . . .** An equivalent phrase to "the wisdom of this age" (v. 6).

understand . . . It is not education or intellect or occupation that yields spiritual insight. There is only one source: the Holy Spirit dwelling within a believer.

has freely given us . . . These gifts of God (v. 9) are not merely for the future but are the present experience of Christians.

v. 13 **. . .** The Spirit provides both understanding ("inward apprehension of profound divine truths"—v. 12) and the very "language that makes conversation about these truths possible" (Barrett).

we . . . Not just Paul and his co-workers but probably all mature Christians (v. 6) have this experience—or at least the potential for it.

v. 14 **The man without the Spirit . . .** In contrast to the spirit-filled person in verse 12 is the person who lacks the Holy Spirit and therefore is blind to the spiritual side of life.

v. 15 **judgments . . .** Not only does the Holy Spirit give understanding but he provides a moral standard by which to evaluate all things.

not subject to any man's judgement . . . Barrett suggests that what Paul means here is similar to what he says in 4:3–5: "human condemnation or acquittal are nothing to him. His only judge is the Lord."

v. 16 **mind of Christ . . .** Paul now shifts to this concept which parallels the idea of having the Spirit of Christ.

SESSION 5
Emotional

We like to think that rationality "makes the world go round." In reality, emotion "makes the world go 'round." We elect our presidents more on how we feel about them than we do on their policies. The reactions of Wall Street are based more on how traders and investors "feel" about the stock market than they are on the object health of corporations. Marriages succeed or fail more on how spouses feel about one another than on the effectiveness of making the relationship better through mutual give-and-take.

Obviously, emotions play an important part in our experience of wholeness. Yet many people never learn to understand, express or use emotions in a healthy manner. These shortcomings interfere with virtually every type of human relationship.

Jesus understood the importance of emotions in achieving wholeness. He also understood both the "up-side" and "down-side" of emotions; that is, emotions could be used either constructively or destructively. As we mature as individuals, we should see our own emotions become more edifying and less self-destructive. In the following studies, Jesus and the apostle Paul give us some guidelines for emotional growth.

OPTION 1

Gospel Study/Healing Feeling

OPEN

STEP ONE: Answer the following questions and share your responses with your group.

1. What makes you angry? When was the last time someone tripped your trigger, or blew your fuse, by pushing one of your "hot buttons"?

2. After coming to full boil, are you more like a gas range whose heat can be instantly shut off? Or are you more like the electric range that takes a while to cool down again to "off"? How do you usually get over your anger?

STUDY

LEADER
IF YOU HAVE
MORE THAN SEVEN
AT THE MEETING,
SUBDIVIDE INTO
GROUPS OF FOUR
FOR GREATER
PARTICIPATION
(SEE BOX ON
PAGE 6).

STEP TWO: Read Matthew 5:21–26 and discuss your responses to the following questions with your group.

²¹"You have heard that it was said to the people long ago, 'Do not murder, and anyone who murders will be subject to judgment.' ²²But I tell you that anyone who is angry with his brother will be subject to judgment. Again, anyone who says to his brother, 'Raca' is answerable to the Sanhedrin. But anyone who says, 'You fool!' will be in danger of the fire of hell.

23"Therefore, if you are offering your gift at the altar and there remember that your brother has something against you, 24leave your gift there in front of the altar. First go and be reconciled to your brother; then come and offer your gift.

25"Settle matters quickly with your adversary who is taking you to court. Do it while you are still with him on the way, or he may hand you over to the judge, and the judge may hand you over to the officer, and you may be thrown into prison. 26I tell you the truth, you will not get out until you have paid the last penny."

Matthew 5:21-26 NIV

1. If your group collected "a penny for your thoughts" every time you got angry this past month, how much would you owe?

2. What did Jesus teach about anger in verses 21-22?
   a. That anger is okay under certain circumstances
   b. That anger interferes with healthy relationships
   c. That anger has no place between brothers/sisters
   d. That anger is a sin and can lead to judgment

3. Why did Jesus quote from the Old Testament here?
   a. Because the Jews placed great importance on it
   b. Because he believed it to be God's word
   c. Because he was trying to show how knowledgeable he was
   d. Because he was building his teachings on an Old Testament base

4. In what ways does our society downplay anger?
   a. It makes anger into "assertiveness"
   b. It sees anger as a natural part of healthy competition
   c. It sees anger as a constructive force in a relationship
   d. It accepts anger as valid in most situations

5. How does anger with our "brother/sister" interfere with our relationship with God?
   a. God "turns off" to us when we are angry
   b. Anger interferes with our ability to approach God with the right spirit
   c. Anger is a sin which must be confessed before we commune with God
   d. We must reconcile our relationship with our brother/sister before anything else can happen

6. What does it mean to "be reconciled to your brother"?
   a. That we ask his/her forgiveness
   b. That we win them over to our way of thinking
   c. That we restore the relationship
   d. That we behave as Christ would have behaved

7. In verses 25 and 26, what is Jesus teaching us?
   a. When we are wrong, admit it
   b. Right wrongs quickly
   c. Avoid court at all cost
   d. Right wronged relationships or be judged
   e. Always admit you are wrong, no matter the circumstance
   f. Getting angry and staying angry can be costly

APPLY

STEP THREE: Answer the following questions and share your responses with your group.

1. Do you currently have one person (or more) with whom you are angry? What is the health of that relationship?

2. What practical steps can you take to restore that relationship?

OPTION 2

Epistle Study/Light-Headed

OPEN

STEP ONE: Start with the OPEN questions on page 36.

STUDY

STEP TWO: Read Ephesians 4:17–32 and discuss your responses to the following questions with your group. If you do not understand a word or phrase, check the Reference Notes on page 40.

17So I tell you this, and insist on it in the Lord, that you must no longer live as the Gentiles do, in the futility of their thinking. 18They are darkened in their understanding and separated from the life of God because of the ignorance that is in them due to the hardening of their hearts. 19Having lost all sensitivity, they have given themselves over to sensuality so as to indulge in every kind of impurity, with a continual lust for more.

20You, however, did not come to know Christ that way. 21Surely you heard of him and were taught in him in accordance with the truth that is in Jesus. 22You were taught, with regard to your former way of life, to put off your old self, which is being corrupted by its deceitful desires; 23to be made new in the attitudes of your minds; 24and to put on the new self, created to be like God in true righteousness and holiness.

25Therefore each of you must put off falsehood and speak truthfully to his neighbor, for we are all members of one body. 26"In your anger do not sin": Do not let the sun go down while you are still angry, 27and do not give the devil a foothold. 28He who has been stealing must steal no longer, but must work, doing something useful with his own hands, that he may have something to share with those in need.

²⁹Do not let any unwholesome talk come out of your mouths, but only what is helpful for building others up according to their needs, that it may benefit those who listen. ³⁰And do not grieve the Holy Spirit of God, with whom you were sealed for the day of redemption. ³¹Get rid of all bitterness, rage and anger, brawling and slander, along with every form of malice. ³²Be kind and compassionate to one another, forgiving each other, just as in Christ God forgave you.

Ephesians 4:17–32 NIV

1. At what age did Mom let you start choosing your own clothes to wear? Is Mom the one who gives you the most new clothes for Christmas, or has another mother figure taken over that role? Who do you consult as to what looks best on you today?

2. How is this clothing metaphor used in this passage to bring out the major differences between Christians and non-Christians? What exactly does it mean "to put off your old self" and "to put on the new self"?

3. In what ways has our society lost "sensitivity" and given ourselves over to "sensuality"?

4. Do you see this process of changing yourself as brought on by supernatural intervention or by a conscious, willful choice?

5. According to these verses, is anger always wrong? Why? Why not?

6. In what practical ways do our emotions enhance or detract from our relationship with God?

7. What negative emotions should we eliminate and what positive emotions should we cultivate?

REFLECT

STEP THREE: As time allows, discuss with your group your agreement or disagreement with the following statements.

- The man who screams at a football game but is distressed when he hears of a sinner weeping at the cross and murmurs about the dangers of emotionalism, hardly merits intelligent respect.

  — W. E. Sangster

- No natural feelings are high or low, holy or unholy, in themselves. They are all holy when God's hand is on the rein. They all go bad when they . . . make themselves into false gods.

  — C. S. Lewis

STEP FOUR: Answer the following questions and share your responses with your group.

1. What part do you think your emotions play in your relationship with God?

2. If you were to change anything about your emotional make-up, what would you change?

3. What specific prayer requests would you offer to help change your "old self" to your "new self"? (Perhaps your group would like to pray for all the member's requests right now.)

Summary . . . Paul continues his exposition of the "life worthy of (our) calling." Having urged the Christians to cultivate *unity* (4:1-16), now he urges them to cultivate *purity* (4:17-5:21). In shifting his topic, Paul also shifts his focus. In discussing unity his focus was on the Christian community. In discussing purity his focus will be on the Christian individual.

vv. 17–19 . . . The Gentile lifestyle is described in a fashion parallel to Paul's more extended exposition in Romans 1:18-32. In both sections the pagan spiral into darkness begins with *hardness of heart* which leads to *distorted thinking* which in turn brings *alienation from God*, out of which flows a *consuming sensuality*.

v. 17 **in the Lord** . . . In the same way by which he began the previous section on unity (see 4:1), Paul begins this new section. He is writing to them not on his own authority but *in the Lord's name*. This is Paul the apostle speaking, not Paul the man.

as the Gentiles do . . . Paul begins this section on purity of life by describing the typical Gentile lifestyle from which Christians must flee. Not every Gentile lived this way, of course. Still, Paul's description of how they as pagans once lived is similar to what Gentile authors were saying. For example, Aristides, a second-century writer, "recites the sins of 'the Greeks' in terms which compel a translator for general readers to leave frequent gaps in the translation" (Moule). As Aristides put it: "The Greeks practice foul things."

the futility of their thinking . . . Paul emphasizes the connection between thought and behavior. By means of three phrases he hammers home his point that Gentiles live as they do because their *thinking* is amiss. He points to "the futility of their thinking," to the fact that "they are darkened in their understanding" and to their "ignorance." Right thinking does matter if a person is to get on with right living.

v. 18 **hardening of their hearts . . .** The center of their being (the heart) has become "stonelike" or "petrified." The word Paul uses is *poros* and it means "marble" or a "callus."

v. 19 **sensuality/impurity/lust . . .** By these three nouns Paul describes what the pagan lifestyle had evolved into. Such forms of over-indulgence (lack of self-control) stand in contrast to the "sensitivity" which ought to characterize life.

vv. 20-21 **to know Christ/heard of him/taught in him . . .** In contrast to the three phrases which describe the wrong thinking of the pagan, Paul sets these three phrases which describe how the Christian comes to learn the right way of thinking. The first phrase, "to know Christ" is literally "to learn the Messiah" and focuses on the fact that Christ is the *subject matter* of their education. The second phrase, "You heard of him" is literally "you heard him" and emphasizes that Jesus himself is the teacher. The third phrase, "you were taught in him" makes the point that Jesus is the very environment within which their learning takes place. The path to right thinking (and hence to right-living) is via the school of the Messiah.

vv. 22, 24 **put off/put on . . .** Paul develops a clothing metaphor here. At conversion the Christian sheds (strips off) his/her old, ragged, filthy garment and puts on a fresh, new cloak.

old self/new self . . . "Every time the singular of the 'man' (self) occurs in Ephesians the 'man' mentioned has a specific relation to Christ. The 'perfect man' (4:13) as well as the 'inner man' (3:16-17) is Christ himself . . . Therefore in 4:24 the 'New Man' (new self) is most likely Christ himself . . . the 'Old Man' (old self) is Adam, the anti-type of Christ (Romans 5:12-21; 1 Corinthians 15:21-28, 45-55)" (Barth). In conversion, therefore, the Christian puts off his/her old, sinful nature and puts on the very life of Christ. However, here the verb is in present tense.

v. 23 **. . .** The verbs translated "put off" and "put on" are in the aorist tense, that is, they signify a completed past action. This exchange of natures occurs at conversion. However, here the verb tense is a present infinitive, "be made new" or "be renewed," indicating the need for ongoing, continual renewal. Once again Paul is saying, "Be what you are."

the attitude of your minds . . . Again, the emphasis is on right thinking in order to be able to live right.

vv. 25–32 . . . Paul now gives a few concrete examples of what this new lifestyle looks like. It is characterized by truth (v. 25), by proper control of anger (vv. 26–27), by honest labor (v. 28), by edifying talk (vv. 29–30), by love (vv. 31–32).

v. 25 . . . This verse is a model for how Paul discusses each of the six topics. He begins with the *negative deed*, in this case, falsehood. (In Greek the word is literally "the lie.") Then he sets in contrast the *positive virtue* which he commends, in this case, truthful speech. Next, he gives a *reason* for this command: here, it is that we are all *neighbors.* In fact, we are even closer than that, "we are all members of one body." Lies destroy fellowship. Unity must be built on trust, and trust comes via truth.

Therefore . . . Having just described what is indeed so for Christians (they have a new self which bears the marks of God's very nature: righteousness and holiness). Paul will now describe specifically what their lifestyle ought to be.

v. 26 **In your anger** . . . Paul recognizes that there is such a thing as legitimate anger. Paul says in 5:6 that God experiences anger (The translation obscures this meaning. Although the phrase in 5:6 is rendered as "God's wrath," the same word is used there which is here translated "anger.") Jesus was angry (Mark 3:5). There are certain situations in which anger is the only honest response. For Christians to deny their anger is dangerous and self-defeating. But once admitted, anger is to be dealt with and so Paul identifies four ways to deal with anger. First, "In your anger do not sin." What is the source of the anger? Is it wounded pride or real wrong? Is is spite or is it injustice? In verse 31 Paul will point out that "unrighteous anger" is to be gotten rid of. Second, "Do not let the sun go down" on your anger, that is, deal with it quickly. Do not nurse anger and let it grow. Thirdly, do not let anger develop into resentment. This is what the word translated as "angry" at the end of verse 26 means. Get the anger out in the open. Be reconciled if possible. Apologize if necessary. Fourthly, "do not give the devil a foothold." Do not let Satan exploit your anger, turning it into hostility, or use it to disrupt fellowship.

v. 28 . . . It is not enough simply to stop stealing; the thief must also start working.

vv. 29-30 . . . From the use of one's hands, Paul turns to the use of one's mouth. The word translated "unwholesome" means "rotten" and is used to describe spoiled fruit (as in Matthew 12:33). Instead of rancid words that wound others, the words of Christians ought to edify ("building others up"), be appropriate ("according to their needs"), bring grace (this is the literal rendering of the word translated "benefit"), and not cause distress for the *Holy* Spirit (by *unholy* words).

v. 31 . . . Paul identifies 6 negative attitudes which must be erased from the Christian life.

bitterness . . . Spiteful, longstanding resentment.

rage and anger . . . These two attitudes are related. The first is a more immediate flare up while the latter is a more long term, sullen hostility. This is not the "righteous anger" Paul dealt with in verse 26.

brawling . . . Loud self-assertion, screaming arguments.

slander . . . Insulting one another behind his/her back.

malice . . . Wishing or actually plotting evil against another.

v. 32 . . . In contrast to the negative attitudes listed in verse 31, here Paul identifies a set of positive attitudes that ought to characterize the Christian. Instead of bitterness, rage, anger, brawling, slander, and malice the Christian is to display kindness, compassion and forgiveness.

SESSION 6
Spiritual

Interest in the spiritual side of life has increased in recent years. A fascination with the occult and Eastern religions has produced a proliferation of New Age bookstores and the addition of an "occult section" to neighborhood bookstores. The resurgence of "the Charismatic Movement" in recent decades has brought a renewed interest in the ministry of the Holy Spirit.

But an attraction to the spiritual side of life is certainly not new. Our earliest historical records indicate that people looked to "a higher power" to find meaning in life. Many centuries ago Augustine wrote, "There is a God-shaped vacuum in every person that only Christ can fill." Today, people are still trying to fill that vacuum—often without Christ.

In the following Gospel Study, we will examine the spiritual claims of Christ. Not only do we see Jesus as a spiritual being who has existed from the dawn of time, but we are also confronted with his earthly purpose and mission. It is through Jesus that we connect with the spiritual. And in the Epistle passage, we see that with the coming of Christ we get the accelerated ministry of the Holy Spirit and the promise that Christ actually dwells in us.

OPTION 1

Gospel Study/Wholly Spirit

OPEN

STEP ONE: Answer the following question and share your responses with your group.

**LEADER:
IF YOU HAVE
MORE THAN SEVEN
AT THE MEETING,
SUBDIVIDE
INTO GROUPS OF
FOUR FOR
GREATER
PARTICIPATION
(SEE BOX ON
PAGE 6).**

Which one of the following statements best describes how you view the spiritual dimension? Why do you think this way?
——— I think it is the most important dimension
——— I think it is over-emphasized
——— I think it is non-existent
——— I think it should be given more emphasis
——— I think that it affects every aspect of life
——— I think it is poorly understood
——— I really don't know much about it
——— I think it is only emotional
——— I think it is confusing
——— I think it brings ultimate meaning to life

STEP TWO: Read John 1:1-18 and discuss your responses to the following questions with your group.

> ¹*In the beginning was the Word, and the Word was with God, and the Word was God. ²He was with God in the beginning.*
>
> ³*Through him all things were made; without him nothing was made that has been made. ⁴In him was life, and that life was the light of men. ⁵The light shines in the darkness, but the darkness has not understood it.*
>
> ⁶*There came a man who was sent from God; his name was John. ⁷He came as a witness to testify concerning that light, so that through him all men might believe. ⁸He himself was not the light; he came only as a witness to the light. ⁹The true light that gives light to every man was coming into the world.*
>
> ¹⁰*He was in the world, and though the world was made through him, the world did not recognize him. ¹¹He came to that which was his own, but his own did not receive him. ¹²Yet to all who received him, to those who believed in his name, he gave the right to become children of God—¹³children born not of natural descent, nor of human decision or a husband's will, but born of God.*
>
> ¹⁴*The Word became flesh and made his dwelling among us. We have seen his glory, the glory of the One and Only, who came from the Father, full of grace and truth.*
>
> ¹⁵*John testifies concerning him. He cries out, saying, "This was he of whom I said, 'He who comes after me has surpassed me because he was before me.' " ¹⁶From the fullness of his grace we have all received one blessing after another. ¹⁷For the law was given through Moses; grace and truth came through Jesus Christ. ¹⁸No one has ever seen God, but God the One and Only, who is at the Father's side, has made him known.*
>
> *John 1:1-18 NIV*

1. If you really wanted to explain to someone how much you loved them, what would you do?
   a. Rent a billboard, radio spot or classified ad
   b. Send a video, singing telegram, or a classic love poem
   c. Use the grapevine and other networks to pass the word
   d. Go yourself, be vulnerable and risk rejection

2. What do we learn about Jesus in these verses?
   a. That Jesus existed in the beginning
   b. That Jesus is the creator and sustainer of life
   c. That we would all be in darkness if it were not for Jesus
   d. That Jesus was God in the flesh who came to earth
   e. That Jesus was the Great Communicator of all time

3. Why did John call Jesus "the Word"?
   a. Because he taught a lot
   b. Because he was the embodiment of Old Testament law
   c. Because he makes the Scriptures come alive
   d. Because he was truth in the flesh
   e. Because he was the living Word of God

4. Why was Jesus also called "the light"?
   a. Because he was bright
   b. Because he brought spiritual enlightenment to a spiritually dark world
   c. Because he had a glow about him
   d. Because he "lit a fire" under his disciples

5. What part did John the Baptist play in Jesus' earthly ministry?
   a. He allowed others to contrast Jesus with John
   b. He prepared the people for Jesus' message
   c. He announced the coming of Jesus
   d. He gave Jesus support

6. Why did Jesus' people reject him?
   a. Because they were expecting a different kind of Messiah
   b. Because they did not want to follow anyone else
   c. Because Jesus was a despised Galilean
   d. Because they were spiritually blind

7. How does one become a child of God?
   a. By deciding you want to be
   b. By joining a church
   c. By receiving Jesus as your Savior
   d. By believing in Jesus' name

8. In what way(s) did Jesus make the spiritual realm believable?
   a. He performed miracles that defied explanation
   b. He spoke matter-of-factly about heaven and life after death
   c. He was God who came to earth as a man
   d. He spoke a message so true that it could only come from God

APPLY

STEP THREE: Answer the following questions and share your responses with your group.

1. How would you assess your spiritual life? (Use any rating scale or illustrative metaphor you want.)

2. What would have to happen in your life to make you a more spiritual person?

Epistle Study/Fully Filled

STEP ONE: Start with the OPEN question on page 44.

STEP TWO: *Read Ephesians 3:14-21* and discuss your responses to the following questions with your group. If you do not understand a word or phrase, check the Reference Notes on page 48.

¹⁴For this reason I kneel before the Father, ¹⁵from whom his whole family in heaven and on earth derives its name. ¹⁶I pray that out of his glorious riches he may strengthen you with power through his Spirit in your inner being, ¹⁷so that Christ may dwell in your hearts through faith. And I pray that you, being rooted and established in love, ¹⁸may have power, together with all the saints, to grasp how wide and long and high and deep is the love of Christ, ¹⁹and to know this love that surpasses knowledge—that you may be filled to the measure of all the fullness of God.

²⁰Now to him who is able to do immeasurably more than all we ask or imagine, according to his power that is at work within us, ²¹to him be glory in the church and in Christ Jesus throughout all generations, for ever and ever! Amen.

Ephesians 3:14-21 NIV

1. How close (geographically, emotionally, and spiritually) is your extended family?

2. Who is God's "whole family in heaven and on earth"?

3. According to verses 16-17, how does the Holy Spirit empower us? How do we get ready to receive this power?

4. How can we begin to comprehend the love of Christ?

5. How can Christ's love help us to experience the fullness of God?

6. What part should the supernatural power of God play in our lives?

7. In what practical ways should the power of God be manifested in our churches?

STEP THREE: As time allows, discuss with your group your agreement or disagreement with the following statements.

• Without the power of the Holy Spirit the Christian life is an exercise in futility.

— Jean Meland

● If a person is filled with the Holy Spirit, his witness will not be optional or mandatory—it will be inevitable.

— Richard Halverson

STEP FOUR: Answer the following questions and share your responses with your group.

1. What has been your experience(s) with the ministry of the Holy Spirit?

2. In what practical ways can the power of the Spirit become more evident in your life?

Summary . . . This section has been called "one of the gems of the epistle" (Mitton) and "the highlight of Ephesians" (Haupt). In it Paul completes the prayer he began in verse 1.

There are three parts to the passage. In verses 14-15, Paul describes his manner of prayer and identifies the recipient of his petitions. In verses 16-19, Paul prays the prayer itself. In verses 20-21, Paul acknowledges the limitations of his prayer.

In the prayer itself (vv. 16-19) Paul asks for two main things—strength and knowledge—via three petitions. In verses 16-17, Paul asks that Christians be given inner strength. In verses 18-19a he asks that they might know God's will (and especially know about Christ's love). In verse 19b he asks that Christians be perfected. In these three sections, he prays "for the work of the Spirit, the presence of Christ, and the manifestation of God's glory in the saints" (Barth).

The focus of 3:14-21 is on the individual believer and his/her ongoing experience of the triune God. This emphasis on the individual nicely balances the previous emphasis (2:11-3:13) on the collective (the Church). Being a Christian involves both individual growth and collective community.

vv. 14-19 . . . In Greek this is all one sentence.

v. 14 **For this reason . . .** Paul repeats this phrase, first used in verse 1, and so picks up again the prayer he began back there. What motivates this prayer and shapes its content is what he said in chapters 1 and 2. There he pointed out God's intention to create a new body (the church) out of old enemies (Jew and Gentile). To be a part of such a company is humanly impossible—unless a person is changed from within. So this is what Paul will pray for. He will pray that God the Holy Spirit will work in their inner being (v. 16), that God the Son will dwell in their hearts (v. 17), and that God the Father will fill them with his fullness (v. 19).

48

v. 14 **I kneel . . .** Jews typically *stood* when they prayed as is seen in the parable of the Pharisee and the Tax Collector (Luke 18:9-14; see also Matthew 6:5 and Mark 11:25). However, in times of great distress or deep feeling one might kneel or lie prostrate. Ezra did this when he heard about the intermarriage between the people of Israel and the surrounding tribes (Ezra 9:3-5). In Gethsemane Jesus "fell with his face to the ground and prayed" (Matthew 26:39).

Father . . . Paul seems to intend this title to have cosmic significance. God is the Father over all, whether they yet know him or not. In 4:6 he will call him "Father of all, who is over all and through all and in all." Thus, in the same way that in 1:4-23 Paul describes Christ in cosmic terms, so here he describes the Father in the same way.

v. 15 **family . . .** There may be some wordplay going on here. "Father," in Greek, is *pater* and "family" is *patria*. This is a family derived from the Father. Fatherhood (paternity) is the focus here. "It may be, then, that Paul is saying not only that the whole Christian family is named from the Father, but that the very notion of fatherhood is derived from the Fatherhood of God. In this case, the true relation between human fatherhood and the divine Fatherhood is neither one of analogy ('God is a father like human fathers'), nor one of projection (Freud's theory that we have invented God because we needed a heavenly father figure), but rather one of derivation (God's fatherhood being the archetypal reality, 'the source of all conceivable fatherhood')" (Stott quoting Armitage Robinson).

in heaven and on earth . . . There are two parts to God's family: those on earth ("the church militant") and those in heaven ("the church triumphant").

name . . . In the early centuries, the act of naming was far more significant than merely giving a child a label to distinguish him/her from other children. Rather, To be named was to be given an identity and purpose. To be called by God's name is to be put under God's power and protection.

v. 16 **strengthen you with power . . .** Paul asks that Christians be fortified or invigorated within by the Holy Spirit. He asks that they experience this awesome power of God about which he has written so eloquently. Having been empowered, then they are able to grasp the awesome love God has for them (v. 19). In other words, inner power makes inner knowledge possible.

inner being . . . By this term Paul may be referring to the deepest part of the human personality where a person's true essence lies. The Greeks thought that there were three parts to one's inner being: reason—by which a person discerns right; conscience—as a result of which a person strives for purity and holiness; and will—from which that person derives the ability to do what he/she knows to be right. Furthermore it would appear that it is via one's inner being that God is experienced. The Holy Spirit moves in power there. Christ dwells there. God the Father works there (vv. 19–20). Certain modern psychologists would argue that there is an interface between the deepest layers of the human unconscious and the supernatural world. In contrast, it may be argued that: " 'the inner man' of Ephesians 3:16 is Jesus Christ himself, rather than a part or function of each man's individual self. In this case the strengthening of man does not depend . . . upon man's openness to the influence of certain transcendental powers. Rather the intimate meeting with a specific partner who comes from outside is decisive. The partner is (according to 3:16–19) Jesus Christ who through the Spirit acts in God's power and makes man strong" (M. Barth).

v. 17 **dwell . . .** There are two Greek words which can be used to describe taking up residency. The first, *paroikeo*, means "to inhabit (a place) as a stranger" or "to live as a stranger" (Bauer). Paul uses this word in 2:19 where it is translated "aliens." The second word which is used here, *katoikeo*, means "to settle down" or "to dwell" and it implies a permanent residency (in a house) as opposed to a temporary stop-over (in a tent). In other words, Christ has come to stay. In Colossians 1:27, Paul states that part of this mystery which now has been revealed is that Christ dwells within us.

faith . . . This is the means by which a person is open to the indwelling Christ.

rooted and established . . . By his choice of these words Paul hints at two metaphors through which the character of love is revealed. The Christian is to be anchored firmly in the soil of love just like a tree. The Christian is also to be set solidly on the foundation of love just like a well-constructed house. (The second word in Greek is literally "grounded.")

love . . . *Agape* love is selfless giving to others regardless of how one feels. Such love is the foundation upon which the Church will grow. Otherwise the newly redeemed enemies would remain enemies.

v. 18 **power . . .** Not only does the Christian need power in order to love but a Christian needs power even to comprehend the love of Christ.

with all the saints . . . Knowing the love of Christ is vital for the whole church. Christ's love cannot, by definition, be known in isolation. Love, to be love, must be experienced and expressed. Love is the fuel by which the Church is sustained and grows.

wide/long/high/deep . . . Paul struggles to express the magnitude of God's love. "Modern commentators warn us not to be too literal in our interpretation of these, since the apostle may only have been indulging in a little rhetoric or poetic hyperbole. Yet it seems legitimate to say that the love of Christ is 'broad' enough to encompass all mankind (especially Jews and Gentiles, the theme of these chapters), 'long' enough to last for eternity, 'deep' enough to reach the most degraded sinner, and 'high' enough to exalt him to heaven" (Stott).

v. 19 **to know this love that surpasses knowledge . . .** Again Paul uses extravagant language to make this point. He prays that they will know what can't be known! God's love is such that limited human faculties can never grasp its fullness (though Christians must strive to do so).

the fullness of God . . . It is possible to translate this phrase two ways. If the possessive (genitive) is objective, then God's fullness refers to the gifts of grace which he gives to people. If it is subjective, then God's fullness refers to that which fills God himself. In fact, it is probably this latter meaning which is intended. Christians are to be filled unto the very perfection of God himself.

v. 20 **. . .** Paul prays because God is *able to do* what is asked. In fact, he is able to do much more than we can either *ask* or even *imagine* (think) because of his great power.

immeasurably more . . . Once again Paul coins his own word, in this case a "super-superlative" (Bruce) that is difficult to translate into English. J. B. Phillips renders this double-compound as "infinitely more." By this Paul intends to convey that given our limited knowledge, we cannot even pray for all that God can and will do for us.

his power that is at work within us . . . This power is within individual Christians and within the body as a whole. This is the power Paul has struggled all along to describe and explain.

SESSION 7
Relational

We have considered the physical, intellectual, emotional, and spiritual dimensions of wholeness. But it is the relational dimension which ties all of these elements together. It is our relationships with God, with ourselves and with others which make our lives whole. Without relationships life would not only be uninteresting, it would also be dehumanizing. Through our relationships we learn what it means to be a created human being.

Some relationships are good and some are not so good. Successful relationships with God and others take work. They do not just happen and central to all successful relationships is love and respect.

In the following Gospel Study, Jesus clearly outlines the importance of love in relationships. While it is easy enough to love those who love us, Jesus calls us to the higher love of even our enemies. In the classic passage of 1 Corinthians 13, we have set before us the inspiring example of Christ's love. We are challenged to love as he loved.

OPTION 1

OPEN

Gospel Study/Love Is Strange

STEP ONE: Answer the following questions and share your responses with your group.

1. Which of the following characteristics are necessary to make a relationship succeed? (choose three)

____	trust	____	submission
____	respect	____	common purpose
____	freedom	____	affection
____	friendship	____	compatibility
____	admiration	____	total agreement
____	sense of humor	____	gentleness
____	acceptance	____	like-mindedness

**LEADER:
IF YOU HAVE
MORE THAN SEVEN
AT THE MEETING
SUBDIVIDE
INTO GROUPS OF
FOUR FOR
GREATER
PARTICIPATION
(SEE BOX ON
PAGE 6).**

2. Describe one relationship you now enjoy, or once enjoyed, which has embodied all three of the characteristics you identified above.

STEP TWO: Read Matthew 5:43–48 and discuss your responses to the following questions with your group.

> *43"You have heard that it was said, 'Love your neighbor and hate your enemy.' 44But I tell you: Love your enemies and pray for those who persecute you, 45that you may be sons of your Father in heaven. He causes his sun to rise on the evil and the good, and sends rain on the righteous and the unrighteous. 46If you love those who love you, what reward will you get? Are not even the tax collectors doing that? 47And if you greet only your brothers, what are you doing more than others? Do not even pagans do that? 48Be perfect, therefore, as your heavenly Father is perfect.*
>
> *Matthew 5:43–48 NIV*

1. As a kid, who was your "Public Enemy No. 1"? Why? Today, who do you find toughest to love? Why?

2. Who is "your enemy" in these verses?
   - a. Anyone who opposes you
   - b. Anyone who is different than you
   - c. Anyone who dislikes you
   - d. Anyone who opposes God
   - e. Anyone you dislike

3. Who is "your neighbor" in these verses?
   - a. Anyone in the world
   - b. Any of your friends
   - c. Anyone you come in contact with
   - d. Anyone who believes like you

4. How did Jesus' teaching concerning our enemies differ from Old Testament teachings?
   - a. He instructed us to love everyone, even our enemies
   - b. They did not differ; they were the same
   - c. He based his teaching on love not law
   - d. He reversed Old Testament teachings

5. Why did Jesus instruct us to love our enemies?
   - a. Because they too are creations of God
   - b. Because he knew it would really confuse people
   - c. Because love is the cornerstone of the Christian life
   - d. Because God loves everyone and so should we

6. What do you think is difficult about Jesus' teaching?
   - a. Loving an enemy is tough, if not impossible
   - b. Nothing about his teaching is really difficult
   - c. It is difficult to love someone who has wronged you
   - d. It is difficult to know what he means by "love"

7. What behavior should distinguish a loving Christian from a loving non-Christian?
   a. Loving God
   b. Loving those who love you
   c. Loving the unlovable
   d. Loving your enemies

8. From where does this type of love come?
   a. God is the source of all love
   b. This love comes through hard work
   c. The Holy Spirit gives us this supernatural love
   d. We experience this love because Christ lovingly died for us

APPLY

STEP THREE: Answer the following questions and share your responses with your group.

1. What would it take for you to build a successful relationship with the person(s) you identified under question 1 on the previous STUDY section?

2. If people loved each other as Christ instructed, how would the world be a different place?

OPTION 2

Epistle Study/Higher Love

OPEN

STUDY ONE: Start with the OPEN questions on page 52.

STUDY

STEP TWO: Read 1 Corinthians 13 and discuss your responses to the following questions with your group.

¹If I speak in the tongues of men and of angels, but have not love, I am only a resounding gong or a clanging cymbal. ²If I have the gift of prophecy and can fathom all mysteries and all knowledge, and if I have a faith that can move mountains, but have not love, I am nothing. ³If I give all I possess to the poor and surrender my body to the flames, but have not love, I gain nothing. ⁴Love is patient, love is kind. It does not envy, it does not boast, it is not proud. ⁵It is not rude, it is not self-seeking, it is not easily angered, it keeps no record of wrongs. ⁶Love does not delight in evil but rejoices with the truth. ⁷It always protects, always trusts, always hopes, always perseveres.

⁸Love never fails. But where there are prophecies, they will cease; where there are tongues, they will be stilled; where there is knowledge, it will pass away. ⁹For we know in part and we prophesy in part, ¹⁰but when perfection comes, the imperfect disappears. ¹¹When I was a child, I talked like a child, I thought like a child, I reasoned like a child. When I became a man, I put childish ways behind me. ¹²Now we

see but a poor reflection as in a mirror; then we shall see face to face. Now I know in part; then I shall know fully, even as I am fully known.
   13And now these three remain: faith, hope and love. But the greatest of these is love.

                                                            1 Corinthians 13:1-13 NIV

1. When did you first "fall in love"? Was it infatuation, or the real thing? How could you tell?

2. To what does Paul compare real love? What is the point of his comparison?

3. What kinds of behavior does a person exhibit when s/he has real love?

4. If we have the love of Christ, what is our attitude and behavior toward evil?

5. Why does "love never fail"? Why then do marriages often fail?

6. In what ways is our understanding of love only partial?

7. Why is love greater than faith and hope, and the cornerstone of all successful relationships?

REFLECT   **STEP THREE: As time allows, discuss with your group your agreement or disagreement with the following statements.**

- One of the ironies of the Christian faith is that love, joy, and giving grows (multiplies) fastest when it is shared (divided) with others. This is the new math of the new kingdom.

                                                            — Mary Hollebeek

- We are born helpless. As soon as we are fully conscious we discover loneliness. We need others physically, emotionally, intellectually; we need them if we are to know anything, even ourselves.

                                                            — C. S. Lewis

APPLY   **STEP FOUR: Answer the following questions and share your responses with your group.**

This exercise is for all those who have ever wondered about love—"Is this the real thing?" Listed below are several clues adapted from Ray Short's book, *Sex, Love, or Infatuation: How Can I Really Know?* These clues distinguish real love from mere infatuation. Based on your experience of loving one particular person (past or present, your choice), place an "X" next to those clues that reveal(ed) to you the true nature of that relationship. Then go back and place an "L" next to those clues that you think reflect *love* (as defined in 1 Corinthians 13) and an "I" next to those clues that you think reflect *infatuation*.

_____ Your main interest is what you can see, hear, smell, taste, or touch of the other person

_____ Your main interest is in a person who *is* beautiful, whether or not s/he *looks* beautiful

_____ You *love* this person for his/her few outstanding qualities

_____ You would *like* this person for his/her many qualities regardless

_____ The more you know, the less you like this person

_____ You find that "familiarity breeds content," not contempt or boredom

_____ You believe in "love at first sight"—instant chemistry

_____ You believe that "love grows slowly"—only out of friendship and only through a long romance or courtship

_____ You believe "the path of true love never runs smoothly"

_____ You believe real love is consistently stable, does not wax or wane

_____ You believe love is disorienting, intoxicating, causing one to lose self-control and fall "head over heels"

_____ You believe love has an organizing, energizing, constructive effect in making you be more yourself

_____ When the relationship ends (ended), you will be (were) able to quickly recover

_____ When the relationship ends (ended), you could never quite get over it

_____ Your whole world revolves around this other person

_____ This new relationship becomes a plus, not a replacement, for all other relationships

_____ You believe "love is blind"—your beloved can do no wrong; your love sees beyond any differences that might divide

_____ You believe "love is honest"—not hiding, but disclosing all faults for the other to see

_____ Your parents and friends do not approve of the relationship, but that only drives you closer together—"us against the world"

_____ Lovers must be friends the same way any two people of the same sex are friends; your lover and your friends have a lot in common

_____ You believe "absence makes the heart grow fonder"—of someone else

_____ You believe "absence makes the heart grow fonder"— of your beloved

_____ You believe "love means never having to say you're sorry"

_____ You believe "unless you say 'ouch,' I cannot know that I am stepping on your toes"

_____ You believe of your love relationship that "one plus one equals one"

_____ You believe that, as a couple, "one plus one equals more than two"

_____ You believe that you've got to change to be loved by her/him

_____ You want the other person to be happy, so much so, that you don't care if you are the one who *shares* in that happiness

_____ You believe you are the only one good enough for your beloved; you are unwilling to give her/him up

_____ The more jealous you are, the more you love your sweetheart

_____ You believe love does not restrict, it releases

Summary . . . In this soaring hymn in praise of love (which has become a classic piece of literature) Paul first points out (vv. 1-3) the primacy of love (in contrast to other religious activities); then describes love itself (vv. 4-7) and ends (vv. 8-13) by pointing out love's enduring quality (in contrast, once again, to other religious activities). As Karl Barth outlines the chapter: "It is love alone that counts (vv. 1-3); it is love alone that triumphs (vv. 4-7); it is love alone that endures (vv. 8-13)."

vv. 1-3 . . . If a person does not love, neither spiritual gifts, nor good deeds, nor martyrdom is of any ultimate value to that person. Love is the context within which these gifts and deeds become significant.

v. 1 **tongues of men and of angels** . . . Ecstatic speech—highly prized in Corinth—is an authentic gift of the Holy Spirit; however, it becomes like the unintelligible noise of pagan worship when used outside the context of love.

gong/cymbal . . . Paul is probably thinking of the repititious and meaningless noise generated at pagan temples by beating on metal instruments.

v. 2 . . . Paul contrasts three other spiritual gifts with love: prophecy, knowledge, and faith.

prophecy . . . Such activity is highly commended by Paul (e.g. 14:1); yet without love even a prophet is really nothing.

fathom all mysteries . . . In Corinth, special, esoteric knowledge was highly prized (1:18-2:16), but even if one knew the very secrets of God, without love it would be to no end. That which makes a person significant (i.e., the opposite of *nothing*) is not a gift like prophecy or knowledge but it is the ability to love.

faith that can move mountains . . . Paul refers to Jesus' words in Mark 11:23—even such massive faith that can unleash God's power in visible ways is not enough to make a person significant without love at its foundation.

v. 3 **give all I possess to the poor** . . . Presumably Paul refers to goods and property given to others but not in love. The point is not: do not give if you cannot do so in love (the poor still profit from the gifts regardless of the spirit in which they are given), but rather that the loveless giver gains no reward on the day of judgment.

surrender my body . . . Not even the act of the martyr—giving up one's very life for the sake of another or in a great cause—brings personal benefit when it is done outside love.

vv. 4–7 . . . By way of definition, Paul tells us what love does and does not do. He defines love in terms of action and attitude.

v. 4 **patient** . . . This word describes patience with people (not circumstances). It characterizes the person who is slow to anger (long suffering) despite provocation.

kind . . . In fact, the loving person does good to those who provoke him/her.

not envy . . . The loving person does not covet what others have nor begrudge them their possessions.

not boast . . . The loving person is self-effacing, not a braggart.

not proud . . . Literally not "puffed up." The loving person does not feel others to be inferior nor does he/she look down on people.

v. 5 **not rude** . . . The same Greek word is used in 7:36 to describe a man who led on a woman but then refused to marry her.

not self-seeking . . . The loving person not only does not insist on his/her rights but will give up what is due him/her for the sake of others.

not easily angered . . . The loving person is not easily angered by others; he/she is not touchy.

keeps no record of wrongs . . . The verb is an accounting term and the image is of a ledger sheet on which wrongs received are recorded. The loving person forgives and forgets.

v. 6 **does not delight in evil** . . . The loving person does not rejoice when others fail (which could make him/her feel superior) nor enjoys pointing out wrong in others.

rejoices with the truth . . . Paul shifts back to the positive.

v. 7 trusts . . . Literally "believes all things," i.e., "never loses faith."

hopes . . . Love does not lose hope.

perserveres . . . Love keeps loving despite hardship.

vv. 8-12 . . . Having described love, Paul once again contrasts love with spiritual gifts, emphasizing this time the permanent quality of love over against the transitory nature of the *charismata.*

v. 8 love never fails . . . In the sense that it functions both now and in the age to come. The *charismata* are relevant only to this age.

cease/be stilled/pass away . . . One says, when God comes again in fullness, prophecy will be fulfilled (and so cease); the indirect communication with God via tongues will no longer be needed (so they are stilled); and since all will be revealed and evident, secret knowledge about God will be redundant (and so pass away). Each of these partial revelations about God are vital in this present age but unnecessary in the age to come.

v. 11 . . . The contrast is between this age (when we are still children) and the age to come (where we are fulfilled).

v. 12 Now/then . . . Paul is thinking of the Second Coming; the flowering of the Coming Age in fullness when God reveals himself, in contrast to the here and now—when, although the Coming Age has been initiated, it is still incomplete.

poor reflection . . . Corinth was famous for the mirrors it made out of highly polished metal. Still, no mirror manufactured in the first century was without imperfections. All of them distorted the image somewhat; this is an apt metaphor for our present knowledge of God: it is marred.

v. 13 remain . . . Charismatic gifts will cease because they brought only partial knowledge of God but three things will carry over into the Coming Age: faith, hope and love.

SUGGESTED READING

The Celebration of Discipline, Richard J. Foster, San Francisco: Harper and Row, 1978.

Fearfully and Wonderfully Made, Paul Brand and Philip Yancey, Grand Rapids, MI: Zondervan, 1980.

How Can It Be All Right When Everything Is All Wrong? Lewis B. Smedes, San Francisco: Harper and Row, 1982.

Love Within Limits: A Realist's View of 1 Corinthians 13, Lewis B. Smedes, Grand Rapids, MI: Eerdmans, 1978.

Pilgrimage, Richard Peace, Grand Rapids, MI: Baker, 1984.

Sex, Love or Infatuation: How Can I Really Know? Ray E. Short, Minneapolis, MN: Augsburg, 1978.

Whollstic Christianity, David O. Moberg, Elgin, IL: Brethren Press, 1985.